Estate Planning and Elder Law Basics: Frequently Asked Questions

Estate Planning and Elder Law Basics: Frequently Asked Questions

Brian H. Bronsther, Esq.

JONES MEDIA
PUBLISHING

Jones Media Publishing
10645 N. Tatum Blvd. Ste. 200-166
Phoenix, AZ 85028
www.JonesMediaPublishing.com

ISBN: 978-1-945849-06-0 paperback
Printed in the United States by Author2Market

TABLE OF CONTENTS

CHAPTER 1

IMPORTANT TERMS AND DEFINITIONS

The following terms are used throughout this book and are briefly described below and more thoroughly explored in the various chapters. A brief explanation of these terms will be helpful in understanding the scenarios displayed herein. In addition, the laws affecting the field of estate planning and elder law are generally State specific. The responses provided herein are from the perspective of a New York resident.

Estate is the compilation of one's holdings at death. Whatever is titled in the person's name at the time of his or her death is considered part of the estate.

Probate is the process of proving the decedent's will in court. It is commenced with the filing of a petition with the Surrogate's Court.

Intestacy occurs when an individual does not have a will and his or her estate must be administered as well.

POA is power of attorney.

Tenants by the Entirety is a common method to hold a real estate title between husband and wife, where title to the property automatically vests in one spouse upon the other's death.

Joint Tenants is a common way to hold real or personal property between two or more persons, where the death of one results in the deceased person's interest in the real estate or personal property vesting in the survivors.

Tenants in Common is a common way to hold a title to real or personal property between two or more persons, where a deceased person's interest in the property passes to his or her heirs pursuant to the deceased person's last will and testament, or if the deceased person does not have a last will and testament, according to intestacy laws.

Real property is classified as real estate, including condominium and co-op ownership.

Personal property is everything other than real property and can be broken down into tangible and intangible property.

Tangible property is defined as property that you can physically touch.

Intangible property is defined as any other personal property, other than tangible property.

Last will and testament or will is a document signed by an individual expressing how he or she desires his or her belongings to be distributed upon their death. A number of rules must be followed for the will to be binding.

Look Back Period is a five year period of time that begins with the filing of the Medicaid application. In calculating the look back period all gifts or transfers of assets made within the five year period are subject to a penalty.

Life Estate is the ownership of real property for the duration of an individual's life.

CHAPTER 2

DO I REALLY NEED
TO PLAN MY ESTATE?

Consider the following scenarios in response to this question:

Scenario A:

Jim and Donna have two children and the following belongings: a house purchased when they were just married, valued at $158,000; two cars (one titled in each of their names); household goods and furnishings valued at around $25,000; and a few collectibles that have been handed down over the years. Jim has an investment account in his name only, valued at $50,000, and Donna has a retirement account valued at $67,000, naming Jim as the primary beneficiary, and a savings account in the amount of $10,000. Jim has a life insurance policy at work, with a death benefit of $50,000. Donna and Jim have agreed that Donna's sister, Gina, should take care of their children in the event that something happens to both of them. Under *no circumstances do they want Jim's parents to be in charge of their children.*

If Jim predeceases Donna, without a will, then under New York law, Donna would inherit the house, as it would be deemed to have been held as tenants by the entirety. But the investment account, car titled in his name, and household goods, furnishings, and collectibles would be shared by Donna and her children. In other words, Donna would not be entitled to all that she was expecting, and the children's share would be held in trust until they reached the age of 21.

Similarly, if Donna predeceases Jim, without a will, Jim might be surprised to find out that he would not be solely entitled to the second car and Donna's savings account.

If both Donna and Jim die without wills, first and foremost, the issue of who will be their children's guardian takes center stage. Without a will, the courts decide. Second, their children would inherit the balance of their estate and be entitled to the same at age 21. This would amount to $360,000 to be split between the two of them, allowing them to spend it on whatever they wished at this young age.

Scenario B:

Reggie and Betty are ages 67 and 63, respectively. Reggie is starting to become somewhat forgetful, and his *family has a history of Alzheimer's disease. They have belongings valued at $250,000. In addition, they own a home valued at $150,000. Reggie and Betty have two children, Julia and Robert. Robert is currently unemployed and receiving governmental assistance.*

With Reggie's memory beginning to fail, in the near future it is entirely possible that he will be deemed to lack the capacity to handle his financial and personal affairs. As such, without a power of attorney, the family will have to undergo the expensive process of obtaining guardianship over his person and property. In particular, this will be necessary to sell the house.

With a properly drafted will, upon the death of either Reggie or Betty, they can insure that their assets are distributed the way they want. Otherwise, it is entirely possible that the laws of intestacy would result in the distribution of some of the assets to Robert, resulting in the loss of his governmental benefits and the waste of their money.

Scenario C:

Seymour is single and 48 years old with no children, but he does have two brothers and one sister. Seymour's parents are deceased. One of his brothers, George, had a drug problem in the past. In fact, George has several judgments against him and is considering bankruptcy.

Without a will, Seymour's money will be split equally among his three siblings. As a result, there is good reason to believe that the money George inherits will end up in his creditors' hands.

With a properly drafted will, Seymour can make sure that George's inheritance is protected from his creditors. The use of an irrevocable trust can insure that the money is preserved for George's benefit.

Scenario D:

Bernie and Gladys have a lovely daughter, Janet, who has been married to Ernie for several years. Ernie is a dreamer. He always seems to have a big deal about to happen, that's going to make them millions, but for some reason or another it falls apart. Ernie has lost thousands of dollars over the years, investing in one scheme or another. Ernie and Janet have not been able to save any money and have three children who will be attending college over the next several years.

Without a will, upon the death of both Bernie and Gladys, their estate will go to their daughter Janet. If something happens to Janet, then the majority of her inheritance will be in her husband Ernie's hands. Who knows if the money will be available for their children's college educations when the time comes?

With a properly drafted will, a trust can be created to supplement Janet and Ernie's living expenses and further secure the principal for their grandchildren's educations.

In summary, if you do not plan for your estate, the State of New York dictates who gets your property. In addition, you will not be able to control who raises your children, should they be minors. Furthermore, your children will be entitled to a share of your estate and at age 21, they will receive it. Whether or not they are mature enough to handle the responsibility. Finally, unintended consequences may take hold, and your hard-earned belongings and assets may end up in the hands of a soon to be ex-spouse or creditor of a child.

CHAPTER 3

WHAT DOCUMENTS DO I NEED TO PREPARE IN ORDER TO PLAN MY ESTATE?

Consider these scenarios in response to this question:

Scenario A:

Let's take another look at Jim and Donna, who have two children and the following belongings: a house purchased when they were just married, valued at $158,000, two cars (one titled in each of their names); household goods and furnishings valued at around $25,000; and a few collectibles that have been handed down over the years. Jim has an investment account in his name only, valued at $50,000, and Donna has a retirement account valued at $67,000, naming Jim as the primary beneficiary, and a savings account in the amount of $10,000. Jim has a life insurance policy at work, with a death benefit of $50,000. Donna and Jim have agreed that Donna's sister, Gina, should take care *of their children in the event something should happen to the both of them. Under no circumstances do they want Jim's parents to be in charge of their children.*

No magic set of documents comprises an estate plan, but there are a few documents that no individual or family should be without. The first would be Jim's and Donna's last wills and testaments ("wills"). The wills would set forth their respective wishes concerning the distribution of their assets upon death, as well as who would be their children's guardian.

In addition to their wills, Jim and Donna also should each have a power of attorney ("POA") and a health care proxy ("HCP"). The POA provides for the appointment of another individual, known as the agent, to act on the other's behalf with respect to financial and personal matters. An enhanced POA expands the agent's authority to include estate and tax matters, in addition to the personal and financial matters. The HCP appoints a third party to serve as the individual's agent to make health-care decisions, in the event the individual is unable to do so.

One additional document also considered part of the basic estate planning package is a living will ("LW"). The LW is merely an expression of an individual's intent to terminate life support in the event the individual is in an unconscious terminal condition, with no hope for recovery. The LW appoints an agent to terminate life support under certain circumstances.

Scenario B:

Let's look again at Seymour, who is single and 48 years old with no children, but he does have two brothers and one sister. Seymour's parents are deceased. One of his brothers, George, had a drug problem in the past. In fact, George has several judgments against him and is considering bankruptcy. Seymour has decided that because of his brother George's past and current problems, if he leaves any part of his estate to George, it would either enable his past drug problem or end up in his creditors' hands. What is a brother to do?

Seymour might consider the use of a revocable trust, in lieu of a will. As a revocable trust is a will substitute, it would prevent George's ability to bring a will contest, as there is no will to probate.

Furthermore, being the loving brother he is, for George's benefit, Seymour could create a contingent trust within his revocable trust to defeat George's creditors. With a properly drafted revocable trust containing spendthrift provisions, the trustee could delay the distribution of George's share of Seymour's estate until some favorable resolution could be reached between George and his creditors.

CHAPTER 4

DON'T YOU NEED A LOT OF MONEY TO PREPARE AN ESTATE?

Reviewing the following scenarios can provide some insight to this question:

Scenario A:

Sally and Fred are recently married and have a baby girl. They currently rent a two-bedroom apartment, and Sally hopes to go back to work in the next month or two. Sally has a 401K valued at $15,000 and Fred's IRA is valued at $5,000. Both Sally's and Fred's parents are alive, but Sally's parents live out of state.

Regardless of the value of your assets, you have an estate. Either you are going to dictate how your assets will be distributed, or the State of New York will dictate. Either you are going to decide who will care for your children, or the state will decide.

In Sally and Fred's situation, without a will, upon their deaths, their assets would vest with their minor daughter, and the courts would decide who would be their daughter's guardian. It is entirely possible that their daughter would be forced to live out of state.

Scenario B:

Let's assume that about five years have passed and Sally and Fred finally saved enough money to purchase a small home. One night they are driving along a slick road, and their car spins out of control. Sally is barely injured, but Fred is severely hurt, diagnosed with a traumatic brain injury, and unconscious. Fred's prognosis is not good, and it is unlikely that he will ever regain all of his facilities in the future. It is decided that he should be moved to a rehabilitation center, located near Sally's parents out of state. Sally's parents have offered to take Sally in during this trying period. Sally and Fred now need to sell the house.

To sell the house, both Fred and Sally have to sign the requisite transfer documents, but in this case, Fred is unable to do so. Sally will have to undergo the painful and expensive process of obtaining guardianship of Fred's property in order to finalize the sale. With the incorporation of an enhanced POA, the transfer would be much easier to accomplish. Furthermore, with an HCP naming Sally the designated agent, she would be in charge of making Fred's healthcare decisions. Fred's parents would not be able to take charge, as they have been known to do in the past.

CHAPTER 5

WHAT WILL IT COST IF I DELAY PLANNING MY ESTATE?

Consider the following scenarios in response to this question:

Scenario A:

Sally and Fred have been married for about five years and have a 5 year old little girl. During the past five years they have been able to save up and purchase a small house. Sally has a 401K valued at $15,000 and Fred's IRA is valued at $ 5,000. Both Sally's and Fred's parents are alive, but Sally's parents live out of state. One night they are driving along a slick road, and their car spins out of control. Sally is barely injured, but Fred is severely hurt, diagnosed with a traumatic brain injury, and unconscious. Fred's prognosis is not good, and it is unlikely that he will ever regain all of his facilities in the future. It is decided that he should be moved to a rehabilitation center, located near Sally's parents out of state. Sally's parents have offered to take Sally *in during this trying period. Sally and Fred now need to sell the house.*

The cost of delay in failing to have a POA is dramatic. The cost of guardianship could be thousands of dollars, not to mention the time delay.

Additionally, without a will, assets titled in only Fred's name will be distributed to Sally and their child, with their child's share being held in trust until she reaches the age of majority.

Scenario B:

Richard and Paula met later in life and have been married for several years. Richard has children from a previous marriage, and Richard and Paula have one child together. Their combined assets are in excess of $1,000,000 and consist of their home, investment accounts, and a vacation home in Florida. Their primary residence is in New York.

Although Richard and Paula have done some basic estate planning and have a simple will, upon their death their executor would have to probate their wills in two states, New York and Florida. A majority of attorneys charge a percentage of the probate assets' value. These fees typically range from 3% to 5%. Thus, the financial cost of probating their estate would exceed $30,000.

With the implementation of a properly drafted revocable trust and the proper funding of the trust, the cost would be significantly less, as assets that are held in the trust pass outside of probate.

Scenario C:

Peter and Mary have been living apart for more than 10 years but haven never gotten divorced. Peter has been living with Jessica for the past 7 years and has just been diagnosed with early dementia. When Peter and Mary were first married, they had each executed simple wills leaving everything to each other.

If Peter is deemed incompetent, any attempt to change his will would be ineffective. Therefore, upon his death all of the assets titled solely in his name will pass to Mary. Jessica will be left with nothing, despite the fact that she lived with Peter for several years. Furthermore, without an enhanced power of attorney, there will be little chance of any further estate planning on Peter's behalf.

CHAPTER 6

WHAT IS ELDER LAW?

Elder law is defined by the client to be served. In other words, the lawyer who practices elder law may handle a range of issues but has a specific type of client—seniors.

Elder law attorneys focus on the legal needs of the elderly, and work with various legal tools and techniques to meet older clients' goals and objectives.

With this holistic approach, the elder law practitioner handles estate planning issues and counsels clients about planning for incapacity, with alternative decision-making documents. The attorney would also assist the client in planning for possible long-term care needs, including nursing home care. Locating the appropriate type of care, coordinating private and public resources to finance the cost of care, and working to ensure the client's right to quality care are all part of the elder law practice.

Elder law encompasses many different fields of law. Some of these include the following:

- Preservation/transfer of assets, seeking to avoid spousal impoverishment when a spouse enters a nursing home
- Medicaid
- Social security and disability claims and appeals
- Disability planning, including use of durable powers of attorney, living trusts, for financial management, a health care proxy and living will for healthcare decisions, and other means of delegating management and decision making to another in case of incompetence or incapacity
- Conservatorships and guardianships
- Estate planning, including the management of one's estate during life and its disposition upon death through the use of trusts, wills, and other planning documents
- Probate
- Administration and management of trusts and estates
- Planning for eligibility for certain Veterans Administration benefits

CHAPTER 7

WHAT WILL HAPPEN IF I DO NOT PLAN FOR MY LONG-TERM CARE?

The following scenarios will be helpful in response to this question:

Scenario A:

Bob is 75 years old. He owns a home worth $375,000 and has investments in stocks, bonds, and cash valued at $250,000. Bob is unmarried and has no children but has a brother and sister, who each have two children. Bob always spoke about his desire to leave his assets to his nieces and nephews. So he went to his attorney, who has represented him for the past 35 years, and drafted his last will and testament, leaving everything to his nieces and nephews. Shortly after having "planned his estate," Bob is diagnosed with Alzheimer's disease and has to enter a skilled nursing facility. Bob resides in upstate New York.

The private pay cost of residing in a skilled nursing facility in upstate New York is approximately $10,000 per month. In Bob's situation, being unmarried, the State of New York requires him to spend down all of his nonexempt assets. That includes almost all of his investments in stocks, bonds, and mutual funds. As you can see, at $10,000 per month, after approximately 25 months all of Bob's liquid investments would have been spent on his care. After he spent down his assets he would be eligible for Medicaid.

Although, under certain circumstances, Bob's home would be considered an exempt asset and not counted for purposes of Medicaid eligibility. However, it would be subject to estate recovery and could be at risk, depending on how long Bob resides in a skilled nursing facility.

Scenario B:

Hank is 72 and Ellen is 69. They have been retired for several years and have started traveling a few times a year to visit their children and grandchildren, who live in nearby states. During a recent visit, their oldest child asked them whether they had made any plans in the event one of them suddenly got sick. Hank and Ellen had not thought much about this, since both of them were in good health. However, they agreed to seek some advice upon returning home, to explore their options.

Hank and Ellen own a home that they have lived in since their marriage 45 years ago. They have checking, savings, and CD accounts totaling $300,000. They both worked most of their adult lives, carefully watching their *expenses and never spending money on unnecessary extravagant items.*

As agreed, Hank and Ellen spoke with an elder law attorney, as they knew they should update their wills and their powers of attorney. They were surprised to learn that they could plan now to avoid running out of money in the future, should they need long-term care either at home or in a skilled nursing facility. With the help of their elder law attorney, they placed $200,000 and their home into an irrevocable trust, and named their children as lifetime beneficiaries of the trust. If needed, their children could take a distribution from the irrevocable trust, rather than using their own money for Hank and Ellen's needs.

The remaining $100,000 would be kept in a revocable trust that Hank and Ellen would use for their living and travel expenses. Ellen would apply for a long-term care insurance policy to provide further protection for them should her health fail (Hank had applied previously but was denied). After five years from the date of transfer, the $200,000 and their home placed into the irrevocable trust would not be counted against them as an available resource.

What if, six years later, Hank had a severe stroke and ended up in a nursing home, unable to use his right arm or leg? Ellen tried caring for him at home but was simply unable to do so. Ellen went back to the elder law attorney for help. Because they had planned ahead and set up an irrevocable trust, Ellen was able to keep all the remaining cash assets in their revocable trust (as the balance of the assets in the trust was below the community resource allowance limits), and Hank was able to qualify immediately for state Medicaid benefits. The irrevocable trust (which had grown to $215,000) remained in place but did not count against Hank as an available resource for Medicaid purposes, since more than 5 years had passed and neither Hank nor Ellen had any direct access to the trust assets.

Ellen was incredibly relieved to know that she did not have to worry about paying for Hank's care and could instead focus on visiting him and supporting him as much as possible. Although Hank was unable to obtain long-term care insurance, she has peace of mind knowing their children continue to manage the irrevocable trust and are ready to help both Ellen and Hank as needed.

Alternatively, had Hank and Ellen not planned ahead, when Hank had a stroke at age 78, the $300,000 in checking, savings, and CDs would have to be spent down, on Hank's care, to approximately $ 119,000.00, under the Medicaid regulations in place at the time. While their home would be protected, since Ellen was still living there, if she were to die the home could be subject to estate recovery by Medicaid.

Without planning ahead it could take nearly two years to get Hank qualified for Medicaid, and the process was incredibly stressful for Ellen and her children. Furthermore, no planning has been done for Ellen, and if her health fails, their remaining assets would be at risk.

Scenario C:

George is 76 years old and his wife has died. He has been retired for several years and has started traveling a few times a year to visit his children and grandchildren, who live in nearby states. During a recent visit, his oldest child asked him whether he had made any plans in the event he suddenly got sick. George had not thought much about this, since he was in good health. However, he agreed to seek some advice upon returning home, to explore his options.

George owns a home that he has lived in since his marriage 45 years ago. He has checking, savings, and CD accounts totaling $300,000. He and his wife prior to her dealth worked most of their adult lives, carefully watching their expenses and never spending money on unnecessary extravagant items.

If George planned early, all the assets he put into an irrevocable trust (including his home) would be protected. Under certain circumstances, any assets left outside the trust could be transferred or turned into an income stream to pay for his care, should his health fail; however, he would still need to qualify for Medicaid, which could be problematic. Just as with Hank and Ellen above, with proper planning, the Medicaid application process would go smoothly and quickly. In addition, an enhanced power of attorney would avoid the need for a guardianship in the event George was unable to make the transfers or sign the Medicaid application himself.

If George did not plan ahead, nearly all of his assets would have to be used to pay for his care.

But if George did some crisis planning and assuming an enhanced power of attorney was in effect, a little more than half of his liquid assets may have to be used for his care, depending on the Medicaid rules in effect at the time. This would leave only a portion of his assets that could be transferred to the children (or to an irrevocable trust).

But what would have happened if George was incapacitated and didn't have a POA? And, if George did not have the capacity to make any transfers or to establish an irrevocable trust, a guardianship proceeding would have to be initiated before any transfers could be made, at significant cost.

CHAPTER 8

WHEN DO PEOPLE BEGIN PLANNING FOR THEIR ESTATE? FOR LONG-TERM CARE?

L et's consider the follow scenarios in answering this question:

Scenario A:

Diana is 32 years of age, a single mother with a daughter who is 4 years old. Diana has some life insurance through work, a small pension, and a few thousand dollars in the bank. Diana's husband is deceased and both her parents and in-laws are alive.

What would happen if Diana became incapacitated as a result of a serious car accident?

If Diana had planned early, she would have had an enhanced durable power of attorney, which would allow her agent to take care of her financial and personal obligations while she was incapacitated. Without it, someone is going to have to apply for guardianship over her property in order to handle her affairs. In addition, she probably would have executed a health care proxy, appointing someone to make her healthcare decisions in the event that she is unable to do so personally. Without the health care proxy or in the event that the incapacity is permanent, then the application for guardianship over Diana would be required.

What would happen if Diana died from her injuries?

If Diana had planned early, she would have executed her will. With a properly executed will, Diana would have provided for the guardianship of her daughter, avoiding any custody fight between her parents and her in-laws. In addition, she would have provided for a trust for her daughter's benefit, so that the trustee could use the monies for Diana's daughter's health, education, support, and maintenance. Without a will in place, the court would require the life insurance proceeds, the pension proceeds, and the money in the bank account to be placed in a guardianship account for Diana's daughter's benefit, under the control of the court.

Scenario B:

Let's assume that Diana is newly married to Jack, who is recently divorced and has two children from his previous marriage, a son, age 7, and a daughter, age 9. Jack is 39 years old. Diana moves into Jack's home, valued at approximately $275,000. Diana's parents recently *transferred to her their camp on Lake Greenfield, which has been in her family for generations, as it was becoming too much for them to take care of.*

What happens if Jack dies unexpectedly, two months after getting married?

If Jack had a will, it would have provided for the orderly distribution of his assets. He could have provided for the house to go into trust, to allow Diana to continue living there, and that upon her either deciding to move out or in the event of her death, it could be left for his children.

Without a properly executed will, the house would be distributed among Diana and his children. Most likely, the mother of Jack's son and daughter would seek to sell the house so that the monies from the sale could be invested for the children's benefit.

Scenario C:

Instead of Jack dying unexpectedly, let's say that after 10 years of marriage, Diana dies from complications after surgery from a car accident. What happens to the family camp? And what about custody of her daughter?

If Diana had a will, she could have named Jack her daughter's guardian, preserving the family unit and avoiding any family disagreements between her parents and her former in-laws over guardianship. The will could have provided for the distribution of the family camp, in trust, to her daughter.

Without a will, fighting between Diana's parents, former in-laws, and Jack could start over custody of her daughter. Furthermore, the family camp would be distributed to Jack and her daughter.

Additionally, if Jack dies intestate before he can execute a will, his assets, including the 50% share in Diana's parents' camp, would end up in his children's hands.

In other words, it is never too early to plan your estate. There is no minimum age. If one does not plan ahead of time, then the State of New York will dictate how your assets are distributed. In addition, the costs associated with guardianship are significantly greater than the costs associated with preparing the basic estate planning documents of a will, health care proxy, and power of attorney.

Scenario D:

Let's assume that Jack was in the car crash with Diana. Unfortunately, Diana died and Jack survived, but not without complications. In fact, Jack has a traumatic brain injury, and it looks like he will never be able to work again and will need care for the rest of his life. This set of facts raises all sorts of questions: How is Jack's care going to be paid for? Who is going to be in charge of Jack's healthcare decisions? Who is going to be in charge of Jack's financial and personal decisions?

If Diana had planned early, a properly drafted will would have provided for the distribution of her assets to Jack, in trust for his benefit. Such a trust could protect the assets from creditor attachment, as well as provide for supplemental benefits not covered by any governmental programs.

Without planning ahead, it is entirely possible that the assets distributed to Jack would have to be used for his long-term care and that family camp would be lost for future generations.

If Jack had planned ahead, a properly drafted enhanced power of attorney would have allowed his agent to take control of his finances and personal affairs, avoiding the need for guardianship proceeding. A properly drafted health care proxy would have allowed his agent to take control of his healthcare decisions, also thereby avoiding the necessity of a guardianship proceeding.

Scenario E:

Bob and Anne are in their early 60s. Bob is 62 years old, and Anne is 60 years old. They have three children, Rich, Ken, and Todd, ranging from 24 to 32 years of age. Bob and Anne have a home valued at $325,000, IRA retirement accounts valued at $175,000, and other *financial accounts valued at $110,000. In addition, Bob has a paid-up universal life insurance policy in the amount of $225,000 and a $175,000 term policy. Anne is the primary beneficiary. They have neglected to list any contingent beneficiaries on the policy. Bob and Anne appear to be in relatively good health and are still employed. Bob hopes to retire in a few years. Let's assume that Bob takes ill unexpectedly at the age of 66 and is required to go into a skilled nursing facility.*

If Bob and Anne had planned early, they may have purchased some form of long-term care insurance, in which case either all of or a portion of the monthly long-term care costs would be covered. In addition, a few years before Bob fell ill, Bob and Anne took some proactive steps and sought the advice of an elder law attorney, who recommended the creation of a properly drafted "asset protection trust." Based upon their attorney's analysis and the previous funding of the trust, together, with the use of their long-term care insurance, Bob and Anne only have to pay a portion of the long-term care costs for a few months, as they wait for the lookback period to expire. Upon the expiration of the lookback period, the assets transferred into the trust are deemed a "non-countable resource," and they will qualify for Medicaid for the portion of Bob's long-term care costs that are not covered.

If Bob and Anne had not planned early, then their investment account and universal life insurance policy would be deemed an available resource for Medicaid purposes and Bob would not be eligible for Medicaid. In addition, if Bob's IRA accounts were not in payout status, then they too would be an available resource. Finally, although their residence would not be deemed an available resource, it may be subject to estate recovery at some point in the future.

CHAPTER 9

WHAT ARE TRUSTS, AND WHY SHOULD I USE THEM?

The following scenarios will be useful in answering this question:

Scenario A:

Let's revisit Bob and Anne from the preceding example. When Bob and Anne were significantly younger, they had a will drafted to provide for the distribution of their assets and the appointment of a guardian for their minor children. Now that their children are all adults, they met with their attorney, and they discussed with him that they were concerned about three things: they had heard that probating a will takes a long time; they were concerned that someone might challenge their will; and they had just purchased a second home out of state. Bob and Anne's attorney suggested that they transfer their assets into a trust.

It was explained to Bob and Anne that there are several types of trusts, but only two broad categories. The first is a trust created while one is alive (more commonly known as a "living trust"). The second is created through someone's will (more commonly known as a "testamentary trust"). A living trust is a "will substitute," in the form of an agreement between the trust creator (sometimes known as the "grantor") and the trustee. The grantor's assets are transferred into the trustee's name by the grantor, for the beneficiary's benefit.

By transferring their assets into the living trust created by their attorney and naming the living trust as the beneficiary of their investment accounts and life insurance, Bob and Anne do not have any assets titled in their names and thus have avoided probate. In addition, since there are no assets to probate, there can be no will to question. Finally, by transferring the second home into the trust, they have avoided probate in another state.

CHAPTER 10

WHAT IS THE DIFFERENCE BETWEEN AN IRREVOCABLE TRUST AND A REVOCABLE TRUST?

The following scenarios will be useful in answering this question:

Scenario A:

Rich and Paula are in their mid-30s and are starting to grow their family. They have one child and another one on the way. Their assets consist of a home valued at approximately $237,000; a retirement account valued at $45,000; other stocks and investments valued at $15,000; life insurance valued at $125,000; and two vehicles. Of foremost concern is the desire to provide for their children and the ability to make changes to their estate plan, as their family dynamics change.

A simple will with children's trust provisions would certainly serve their needs. However, the use of a properly drafted revocable trust could create the same result, with the added benefit of avoiding probate. The revocable trust can be changed by simple amendment and, in fact, can be revoked. With the execution of a simple amendment, beneficiaries can be added, changed, and or removed, children's trust terms can be modified, and even successor trustees can be changed.

Scenario B:

Let's assume that time has marched on. Rich and Paula are now in their mid- to late 60s, and their children are all adults, starting their own families. When asked about their estate planning goals, Rich and Paula respond that they want to preserve their assets for their children and to provide for their grandchildren's educations. The value of their estate has increased significantly over the years, and they are conservatively worth $950,000.

Having expressed the desire to preserve their assets, Rich and Paula want to make sure that the expensive costs associated with long-term care does not affect them. The use of an irrevocable trust can certainly work to their advantage. A properly drafted irrevocable trust will stop their creditors from seizing their assets. However, once implemented, the ability to make changes is severely limited.

In other words, the revocable trust can be freely added to, altered, amended, and even revoked. In contrast, under most circumstances the irrevocable trust cannot. However, it should be noted that a properly drafted irrevocable trust can provide for some flexibility, with the use of "decanting provisions", "lifetime benefi- ciaries" and a "limited power of appointment." Finally, an irrevocable trust is more commonly used as an "asset protection trust."

CHAPTER 11

WHAT IS A POA?

Consider the following scenarios in response to this question:

Scenario A:

Lisa and Paul are in their mid-30's and have a baby girl, two years of age. Paul is a truck driver and is out of town for days at a time. Paul and Lisa have a savings account in their own names and a joint checking account. Lisa has a part-time job, and her wages are deposited directly into her savings account, and Paul's wages are deposited into his savings account. In the normal course of their lives, Paul and Lisa transfer money into their joint checking account to pay their bills.

Unexpectedly, Paul gets stuck out of town and is unable to transfer his share of their monthly expenses.

If Paul had a properly executed power of attorney, naming Lisa as his agent, she would have the power to transfer money from his savings account into their joint account. The rent and his credit card bills would get paid on time.

Without a properly executed power of attorney, the rent gets paid late, resulting in a late fee. In addition, because his credit card bills are paid late, the credit card companies report his late payments, damaging his credit score.

While Paul is stuck out of town, Lisa has to go out of town to help her sick mother. Lisa is unable to take care of paying their bills.

With a properly executed power of attorney, naming a successor agent, if the primary agent is unavailable, then either of their successor agents would have the power to take care of their monthly expenses.

Scenario B:

Peter is 72 years of age, and Judy is 69 years of age. They own their home, valued at $225,000, and they have joint a joint savings account with $15,000. They have separate retirement accounts. Peter's is worth $195,000, and Judy's is worth $105,000. They have a joint investment account valued at $150,000.

After having met with their attorney several years ago, they updated their wills to provide for their adult children, but did not do any other estate planning. While Peter was walking the dog, he felt ill, and by the time he got home he was having a stroke. Judy rushed him to the hospital, but not before Peter had slipped into a coma. The doctor's prognosis was not good, and the possibility of recovery was unlikely. After several months of treatment, Judy thought it best for them to sell their home and move into a one-floor apartment.

If Peter and Judy had planned early, a properly executed enhanced POA would allow Judy to sell the house. Furthermore, with a properly executed enhanced POA, Judy can effectuate an asset protection plan, by transferring assets in order to protect and preserve them, while qualifying Peter for Medicaid.

Without a properly executed enhanced POA, Judy would have to seek the assistance of an attorney to obtain guardianship over Peter, so she could sell the property. The cost of bringing a guardianship proceeding is significantly more than the cost of preparing an enhanced POA. Also, Judy would be unable to effectuate the transfer of assets in order to qualify for Medicaid and would thus be required to spend down the assets.

CHAPTER 12

HOW CAN I PROTECT MY CHILDREN IN MY ESTATE PLAN?

The following scenarios will be useful in answering this question:

Scenario A:

Michael and Sara, ages 44 and 42 respectively, have been married 18 years. They have three children, William, Julia, and Joseph. William is 15, Julia is 12, and Joseph is 7 years of age. Joseph was diagnosed with autism. Michael and Sara's assets include their home, valued at $325,000; stock investments valued at $150,000; term life insurance through work at three times salary, valued at $270,000; and Michael has a universal life insurance policy, valued at $500,000.

Michael and Sara have been concerned about the following: guardianship for their minor children, the age their estate will be distributed to their children, protecting their estate from long-term healthcare costs, and preserving *the assets that would be distributed to their special needs child.*

Tragically, while going out for dinner one night, Michael and Sara died unexpectedly in a car accident.

If Michael and Sara had planned early, they would have properly executed wills providing for the guardianship of the minor children; creating a trust for William and Julia, whereby their health needs, education, comfort, and support would be handled; and establishing a special needs trust for Joseph, so he could have the benefit of governmental assistance.

With a children's trust in place, Michael and Sara could provide for the distribution of monies at varying intervals, as their children reached certain ages and accomplished certain academic feats. In addition, the monies would be available in case of a health crisis or other type of emergency.

With a special needs trust in place, monies would be available for Joseph's supplemental needs, those needs not covered by the governmental assistance he was receiving.

Without planning early, the guardianship issue would be foremost, together with the creation of a court-ordered bank account strictly controlled and encumbered by state law.

Scenario B:

Minor children are not the only ones who need protection. Sometimes adult children need protection as well. Let's assume that Michael and Sara survive the car accident and continue to live productive and fulfilling lives. Their children are all grown and are considered adults. However, they recognize that Joseph, their youngest child, has never be able to support himself without assistance. In addition, William's independently owned real-estate company is facing hard times and struggling financially.

If Michael and Sara took some proactive steps, they could have created a supplemental needs trust for Joseph, which could be funded upon their deaths. This type of trust would preserve and protect Joseph's inheritance and allow the funds to be used to supplement the monies he was receiving from the government. Also, Michael's and Sara's wills could incorporate trust provisions providing for William's share of his inheritance to be preserved and protected during his financial struggles.

Without taking the necessary proactive steps, upon Michael's and Sara's deaths, Joseph's share of the inheritance would have to be spent before he would be eligible for government assistance, and William's inheritance would be subject to his creditors' collection efforts.

If Julia developed early onset dementia, what would happen to her inheritance?

If Michael and Sara had met with a seasoned estate planning attorney, they would have incorporated into their wills provisions for this unfortunate contingency. They could have incorporated a contingent supplemental needs trust. Without such proactive planning, Julia's inheritance would be spent on her basic necessities, in lieu of the government financial assistance, and there would be little money for her supplemental needs.

CHAPTER 13

DO I NEED AN ATTORNEY TO DRAFT MY ESTATE PLAN?

N o, but the saying "you get what you pay for" has never been more true than in the field of estate planning. Let's consider the following scenarios in response to this question:

Scenario A:

Daniel is 62 years old, and Jeannie is 58 years old. Daniel is nearing retirement age, and he will receive a nice pension, approximately $75,000 per year, and will probably seek some part-time consulting work. Jeannie plans to work another several years before she retires. Their combined assets consist of a home valued at approximately $325,000; retirement and other investments valued at $450,000; life insurance valued at $350,000; and household goods and belongings valued at $50,000. They have three adult children, Richard, Deborah, and Allie. All three children are employed and earn respectable livings. Richard is married, with a *child on the way. Debbie is engaged, and her husband is a musician. Allie is single and loves to travel.*

If Daniel and Jeannie use one of those "cookie cutter" wills that you find in the form books, it will most likely be designed to leave everything to each other upon the death of either spouse, and upon the second spouse's death to pass to their children equally. In addition, they will probably execute a durable power of attorney and a basic health care proxy. Sounds fine, right? But what happens if either of them develops a debilitating mental illness and needs care, or one of their children prede-ceases them? Their assets may end up being used for long-term care costs or even end up in the hands of their grandchildren when they turn 21 years old.

With a properly drafted will, all of the devastating costs associated with long-term care could be avoided. Also, proactive planning could establish grandchildren trusts, so the funds will be available for their college edu-cations. Furthermore, with a properly drafted enhanced power of attorney, if either Daniel or Jeannie became mentally incapacitated, the other would be vested as the attorney-in-fact and could create an effective asset protection plan, preserving their home and life savings for their loved ones.

Finally, certain formalities must be adhered to in order for a person's will to be valid. There is a significant chance that without an attorney's guidance, either Dan-iel's will or Jeannie's will could be invalid, which would result in a distribution of their assets to the surviving spouse and their children in equal shares, a result they did not intend.

CHAPTER 14

WHAT'S THE BIG DEAL ABOUT LONG-TERM CARE?

C onsider the following scenarios in answering this question:

Scenario A:

Tom and Crystal are 78 and 74 years old, respectively. They have two children, Jennifer and Ron, ages 46 and 43, respectively. They also have three beautiful grandchildren. Tom and Crystal have a home valued at $330,000, a modest retirement account currently valued at $175,000, and other investments valued at $90,000. They have two vehicles titled in Tom's name.

Let's consider what would happen if Tom developed a severe case of dementia, and Crystal was unable to care for him. The family decided that Tom would move into a skilled nursing facility, where he could get the type of care he needed. Much to their surprise, Tom and Crystal found out that Tom's care will cost approximately $9,000 per month. So you can see that in a very short period of time, approximately 10 months, their other investments will be depleted, and they will have to rely on their retirement monies to pay for Tom's care. In addition, if Tom's stay at the skilled nursing facility became an extended stay, the cost of Tom's care would eat up their retirement monies very quickly (almost another year and a half before it would be gone), and they would have to sell their house to cover the costs. Their dreams of having a comfortable retirement and leaving a legacy for their children and grandchildren would vanish.

However, let's further consider what would happen if they applied for Medicaid. Unfortunately, for the past 6 years, Tom and Crystal, being good grandparents, had been gifting their three grandchildren $9,000 each, every year, into a college education account. One may think this extravagant, but from Tom and Crystal's perspective, they knew they had sufficient income from their pensions, Social Security, and retirement to live modestly for the rest of their lives. However, upon applying for Medicaid, the Department of Social Services will apply the 5-year lookback period. In this situation, the Department of Social Services could take the position that Tom had given away $135,000 ($9,000 per grandchild for 5 years), a 14-month penalty period would be enacted, meaning that Tom would be ineligible for Medicaid during that time frame. For Tom's care, Tom and Crystal would be required to spend approximately $135,000 from their retirement and other savings. This would depleat their other savings and reduce retirement savings from $175,000 to $127,000. This reduction in the principal of their savings could reduce the income that Crystal was expecting from their retirement.

Furthermore, even if Tom's stay at the skilled care facility were more short term, Tom and Crystal did not consider what would happen if both of them needed to go into a skilled nursing facility. Then they would go through their savings much faster, spending approximately $18,000 per month.

After the penalty period expires, Tom and Crystal would be eligible for Medicaid. Tom, being a Medicaid applicant, would be allowed to keep one vehicle titled in his name, and they would be able to keep their home, as it is Crystal's intention to continue to reside there. However, these assets would be subject to estate recovery by the Department of Social Services upon their deaths, to the extent that they received Medicaid benefits.

With some proactive planning Tom and Crystal's situation could have been completely different. They could have preserved their retirement, life savings, and home from the devastating costs of long-term care. They would have been able to leave their home and life savings to their children and grandchildren.

Tom and Crystal should have prepared an asset protection trust. With the properly drafted asset protection trust and proper funding and timing of that trust, they could have protected their assets from the effects of long-term care and preserved their assets for their children and grandchildren.

CHAPTER 15

CAN'T I JUST GIVE AWAY ALL MY ASSETS AND PROTECT THEM FROM LONG-TERM CARE COSTS THAT WAY?

The following scenarios will be helpful in answering this question:

Scenario A:

Doug was married to Marie, who died a couple of years ago. Doug is 78 years of age. He has a house valued at $325,000 and savings and investments valued at approximately $215,000. He recently updated his last will and testament, but his attorney did not discuss any alternatives with respect to gift planning or long-term care planning. Doug has read a few online articles about those topics, but nothing very extensive. He is concerned about long-term care costs but has figured that he will just give away his assets. He figures that there is plenty of time. Doug and Marie had one child, Steven, who is 44 years old.

Nobody has the ability to predict the future. Doug does not know, with any degree of certainty, when or if he might become ill. The probabilities are such that Doug will become disabled well before he dies and will undoubtedly need long-term care services. In particular, he may need the services of a skilled nursing facility. Therefore, the responsible act is to plan.

Scenario B:

Doug schedules a meeting with his attorney of 40 years. His attorney has helped him on numerous occasions, but he is not an elder law attorney. Now let's assume that Doug went back to his attorney, who has him transfer his home to Steven. In addition, Doug's attorney suggests that he transfer his savings and investment accounts to Steven. Doug takes his attorney's advice and transfers his home and financial accounts. Four years later Doug has a stroke and must enter a skilled nursing facility.

Doug must consider the Medicaid application and approval process. Although Steven has made it abundantly clear that his father can stay in the house for as long as he can and that his investment and savings accounts are available when and if he needs them, Medicaid requires the production of all financial accounts and records for a 5-year period prior to the application date. This is called the lookback period. Then the amount of all uncompensated transfers of assets within the 5 years is totaled. This sum is divided by the average cost of a skilled nursing facility for the region within which you live. This result produces the penalty period. The penalty period is the time frame during which an individual is ineligible for Medicaid.

So with the average cost of Medicaid in the region where Doug lives being $10,000 per month, Doug's transfer of his house and financial accounts to his son results in a 54-month penalty period being imposed. Medicaid would add up all of the uncompensated transfers, Doug's transfer of the house, plus investments and savings, totaling $540,000, and divide it by the $10,000 monthly cost of regional care. Therefore, Doug would be ineligible for Medicaid services during that 54 month period.

If Doug had met with an elder law attorney, proactive steps could have been taken to avoid this result.

CHAPTER 16

WHAT CAN HAPPEN IF I GIVE AWAY MY ASSETS?

Consider the following scenario in response to this question:

John is 79 years of age, and Marie is 75 years of age. They have a house valued at $425,000 and savings and investments valued at approximately $275,000. When John and Marie purchased the house they only paid $175,000. They recently updated their last wills and testaments, but their attorney did not discuss any alternatives with respect to gift planning or long-term care planning. They have read a few online articles about those topics, but nothing very extensive. They are concerned about long-term care costs but have figured that they will just give away their assets. They have gone back to their attorney, who has them transfer their home to their son, Peter, age 40. He also suggests that they add Peter's name to their savings accounts and investment accounts.

If John and Marie die a few or even several years after the transfer and the addition of Peter's name to their bank and investment accounts, Peter would be considered the accounts' sole owner. With the house having been previously transferred, John and Marie would have successfully avoided probate of their estate.

Alternatively, if prior to John's and Marie's death, let's consider what would happen if Peter caused a terrible car accident and is sued for more money than his insurance covered. If Peter lost this lawsuit, his assets, including John and Marie's house, would be at risk.

What would happen if Peter lost his job and could not afford to meet his monthly expenses? If he filed for bankruptcy, he would be required to list his mother and father's house and bank accounts. This would subject those assets to his creditors.

Let's further consider what would happened if Peter died unexpectedly. Peter's estranged wife and children would inherit John and Marie's house. Effectively, John and Marie could have the house sold out from underneath them. The use of a simple life estate could have protected them from the unwanted sale of their home, notwithstanding the fact that Peter's wife and children would inherit the house.

With outright transfers such as those described above, John and Marie have lost a significant amount of control over their assets. They are dependent on Peter to do the right thing. Had John and Marie used a variety of trusts, both revocable and irrevocable with certain safeguards, they could have avoided probate. They also would have created a situation enabling them to preserve their assets for their use and protect their assets from the devastating costs of long-term care.

Finally, there are significant tax considerations to think about before giving away your assets. In particular, you should consider the capital gains tax effect. If John and Marie give their home to Peter, Peter takes on their tax basis in the property. In this case, assuming no significant improvements, $175,000 will be Peter's tax basis in the property. When Peter sells the house, his capital gains tax will be calculated based upon his tax basis in the property. Assuming a capital gains tax rate of 15%, Peter's capital gains tax would be calculated by subtracting his basis from the sale price ($425,000 - $175,000), giving Peter a capital gain of $250,000. With a 15% capital gains tax rate, Peter would owe $37,500. Instead of giving their home to Peter, if he is the beneficiary of the property, under a last will and testament or a "grantor" trust, then his tax basis in the property becomes the fair market value of the property on the date of death, when he inherits the property. Therefore, there would be no capital gain and no taxes owed. Peter would save $37,500.

CHAPTER 17

WHAT IS PROBATE AND HOW LONG DOES IT TAKE?

Consider the following scenario in answering this question:

Ken and Julie have been married 15 years. Ken is 46 years old, and Julie is 44 years old. They have two children, Mark and Alice, ages 16 and 10 respectively. Ken and Julie own a home in Saratoga Springs, New York, and a condominium in Boca Raton, Florida. They have stock investments of $325,000 and IRA accounts of $125,000 and $195,000, respectively. Ken has a $250,000 universal life insurance policy, and Julie has a $300,000 term life insurance policy through work. They own their home and condo as tenants by the entirety. Their stock investments are held jointly. Their respective IRAs and life insurance policies name each other as the primary beneficiary and their children equally as secondary beneficiaries. Several years later, Ken and Julie divorced. Several months after the divorce, Ken is snowmobiling in the upper Adirondacks and crosses what he thinks is a field, but unfortunately it is a semi frozen lake. He falls through the ice and drowns. Prior *to his death, Ken had met with his attorney and revised his last will and testament.*

A couple of months after Ken's death, his son Mark schedules an appointment with his father's attorney to discuss his father's estate. Mark finds out that prior to his father's death, his mother became the sole owner of the home in Saratoga Springs, New York, and his father became the sole owner of the condominium in Boca Raton, Florida. His mother and father had split the stock investments, and they each kept their respective IRAs and life insurance policies. Ken's attorney explains that they are going to have to probate his father's will. He pulls out his father's original last will and testament and starts to review it with Mark. He explains that the process calls for a petition to be prepared and the executor must sign it. Then it is filed with the court, along with some additional documents. The court, upon review of the documents filed, will appoint an executor to oversee the distribution of Ken's assets. The process to be appointed executor can take a few weeks. Once appointed, the executor must gather the assets and liquidate them, to the extent necessary to pay off Ken's debts. Then the executor can distribute the remaining assets and proceeds among the distributees set forth in the will.

Ken's attorney explains to Mark that the process will take at least seven months, as creditors of the estate have the right to file a claim within that seven-month period. Also, if the assets are distributed prior to that time, the executor would be personally liable for the estate's debts.

Mark finds out that not all of the assets will have to go through probate—only those assets that were held solely in his father's name and did not have a designated beneficiary. In other words, just the condominium, because the stock investments, IRA, and life insurance all named Mark and his sister Alice as beneficiaries. Fortunately, Ken had made that change after the divorce.

It should be noted that if Ken had gone to an attorney who focused on estate and elder law planning, that attorney probably would have advised that his last will and testament contain a children's trust, which would have established the planned distribution of his assets over several years, rather than having everything distributed to his children upon them attaining the age of 21. In addition, the attorney could have suggested that the beneficiaries of the investments, and life insurance would have been the trust contained in the will. For taxes purposes, the IRA could have been rolled over to his children tax free.

****

Needless to say the fields of estate planning and elder law is a complex one and is very fact driven. The author firmly believes that there really is no such thing as a "stupid" question. In fact, the only "stupid" question is the unasked question. It is the author's hope that the foregoing questions, scenarios and responses help shed some light on this ever changing area of the law.

Planning ahead and seeking the advice of a seasoned estate planning or elder law attorney is well worth the time. The author is happy to assist seniors and their loved ones with their estate planning goals and elder law issues. Helping families preserve and protect their family home and life savings from the devastating costs of long term care is a priority. Please feel free to contact the author at www.bronstherlaw.com.

ABOUT THE AUTHOR

Brian H. Bronsther has practiced law since 1984. A graduate of the University of Miami School of Law, he began his practice in Fort Lauderdale. He then moved to Manhattan to practice law. He has practiced in Albany, Latham and the Capital Region for more than 25 years. Prior to founding his own firm he served as General Counsel to Income Property Associates, Inc. In this position, he gained substantial insight into the practical aspects of real estate investment and business.

Today, Mr. Bronsther focuses his practice on estate planning, probate and administration, elder law and Medicaid planning, and business succession planning. Within each of these areas Mr. Bronsther provides detail-oriented, skilled representation and personal client service. He was also a past President of the Capitol Region Bankruptcy Bar Association. He does pro bono work for the Legal Project in Albany, New York.

He is an active member of his synagogue and has served in numerous leadership positions, including President of Congregation Gates of Heaven. In addition to being a lawyer, Mr. Bronsther is an avid tennis player, skier and reader. He is in the process of writing two books. In addition to this book, Mr. Bronsther has started a new book on estate planning for young professionals. In addition to representing businesses, families and individuals across the Capital Region, Mr. Bronsther plans on opening a satellite office in South Florida in the near future.

www.ingramcontent.com/pod-product-compliance
Lightning Source LLC
Chambersburg PA
CBHW022108210326
41521CB00029B/336